AF256142

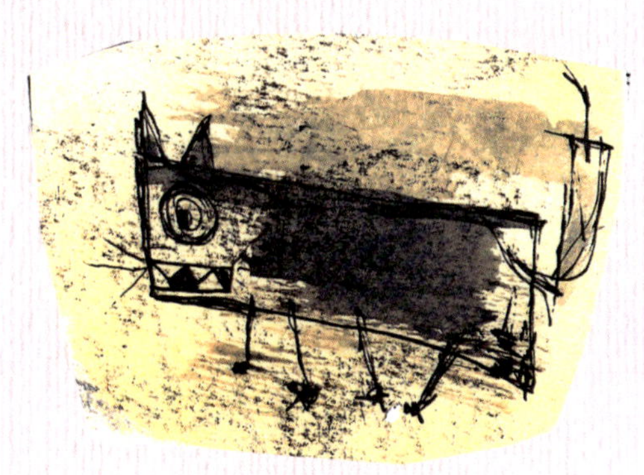

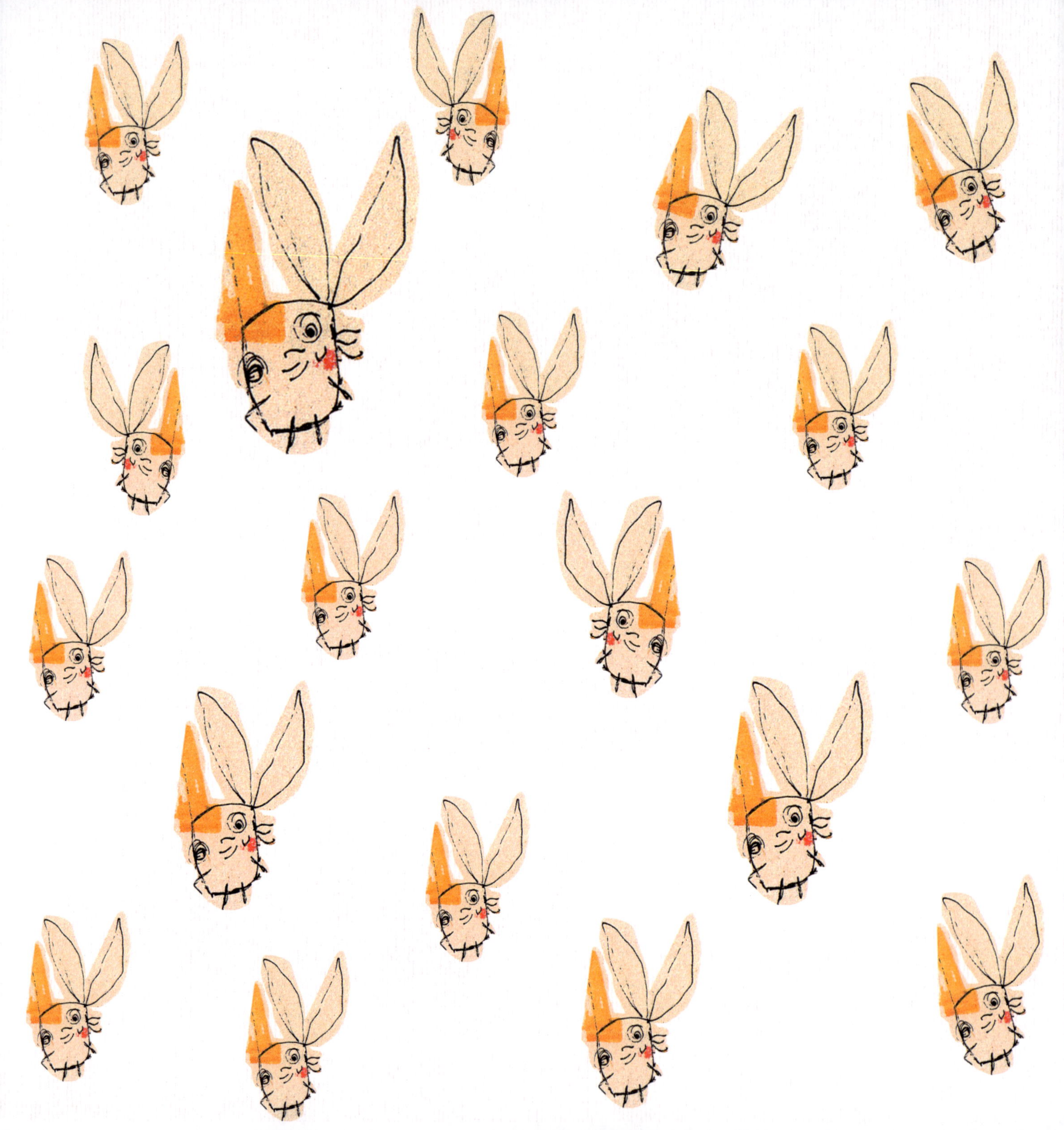

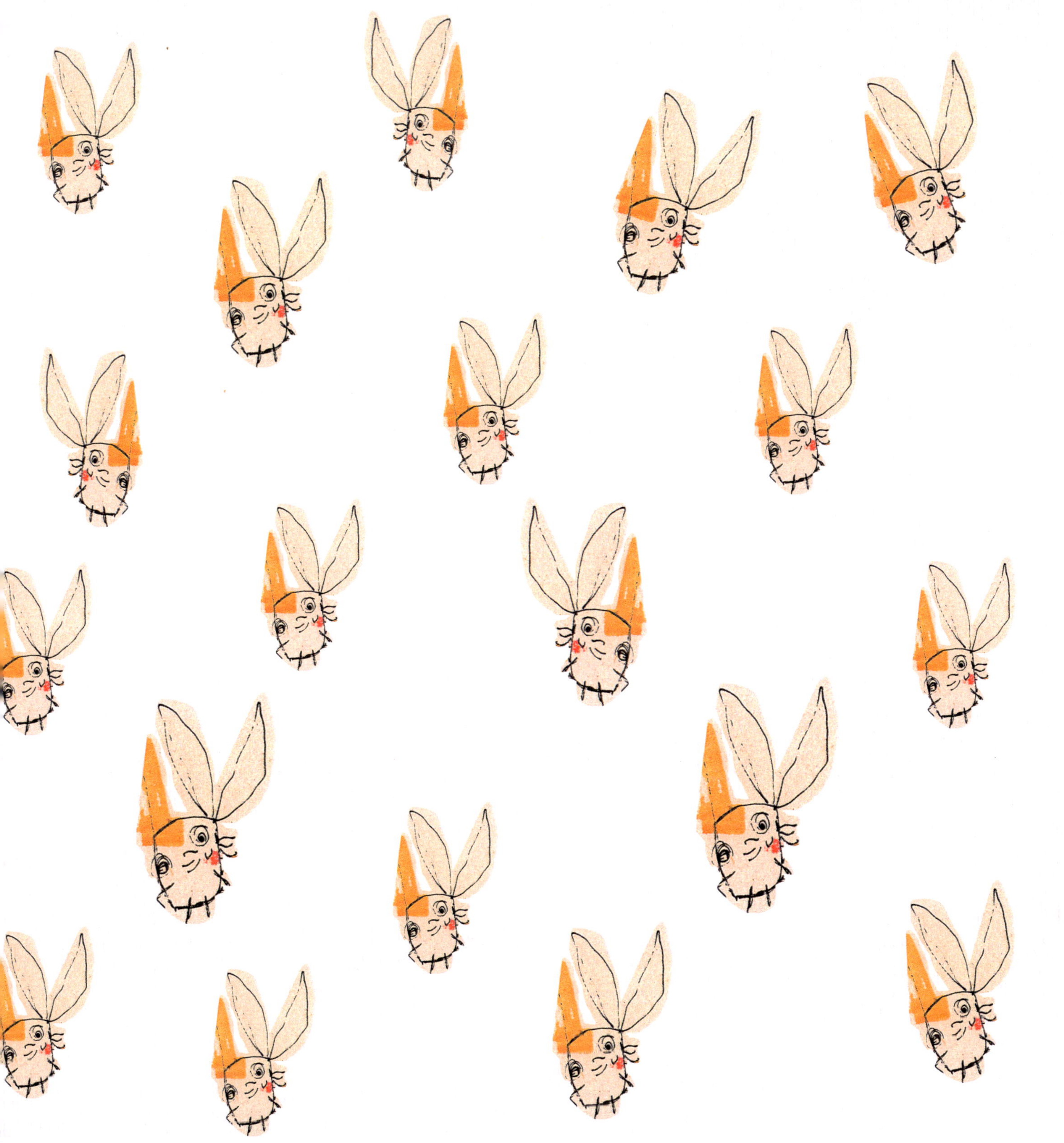

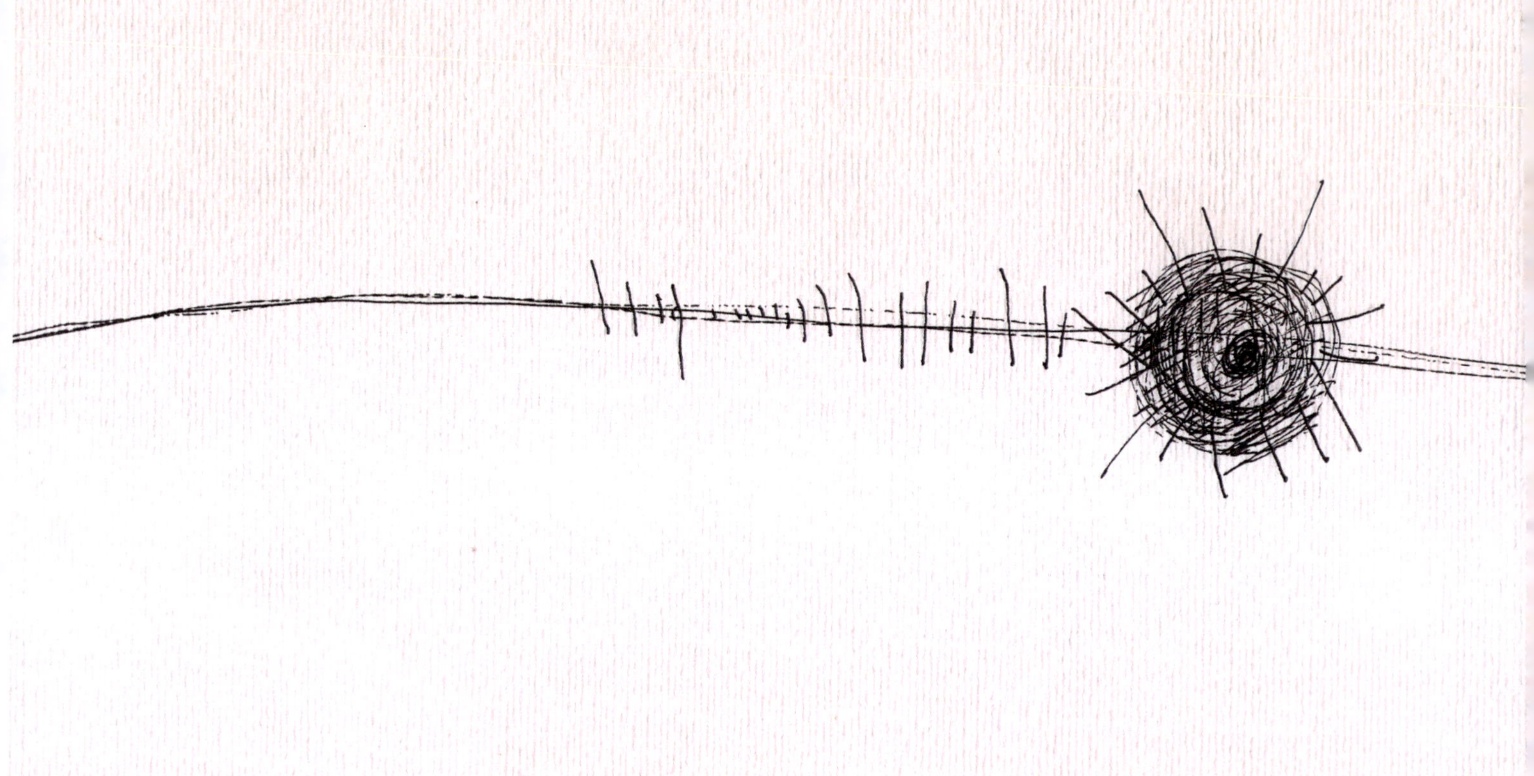

THE RABBIT

BAHAR TAGHIANI

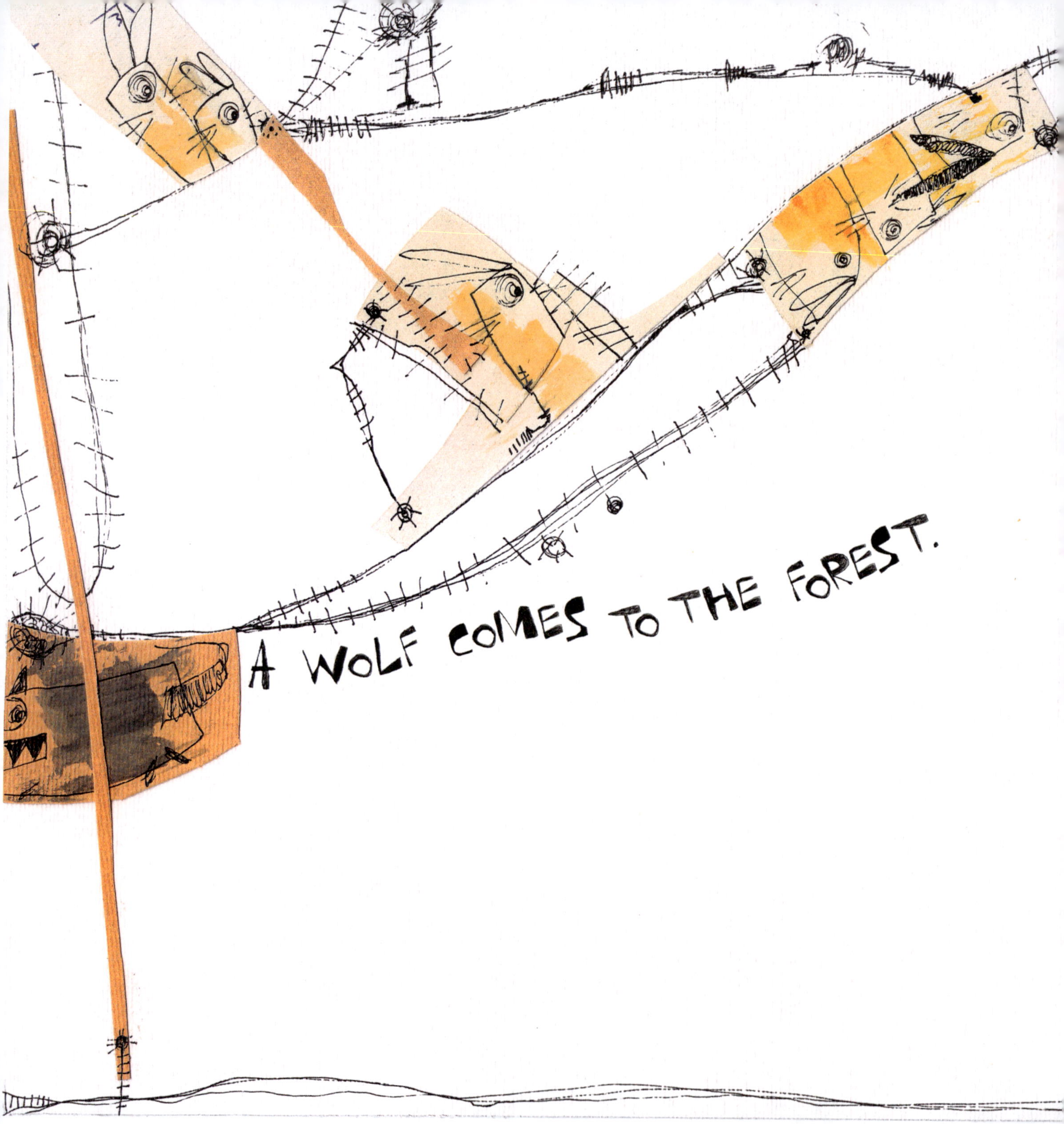

A WOLF COMES TO THE FOREST.

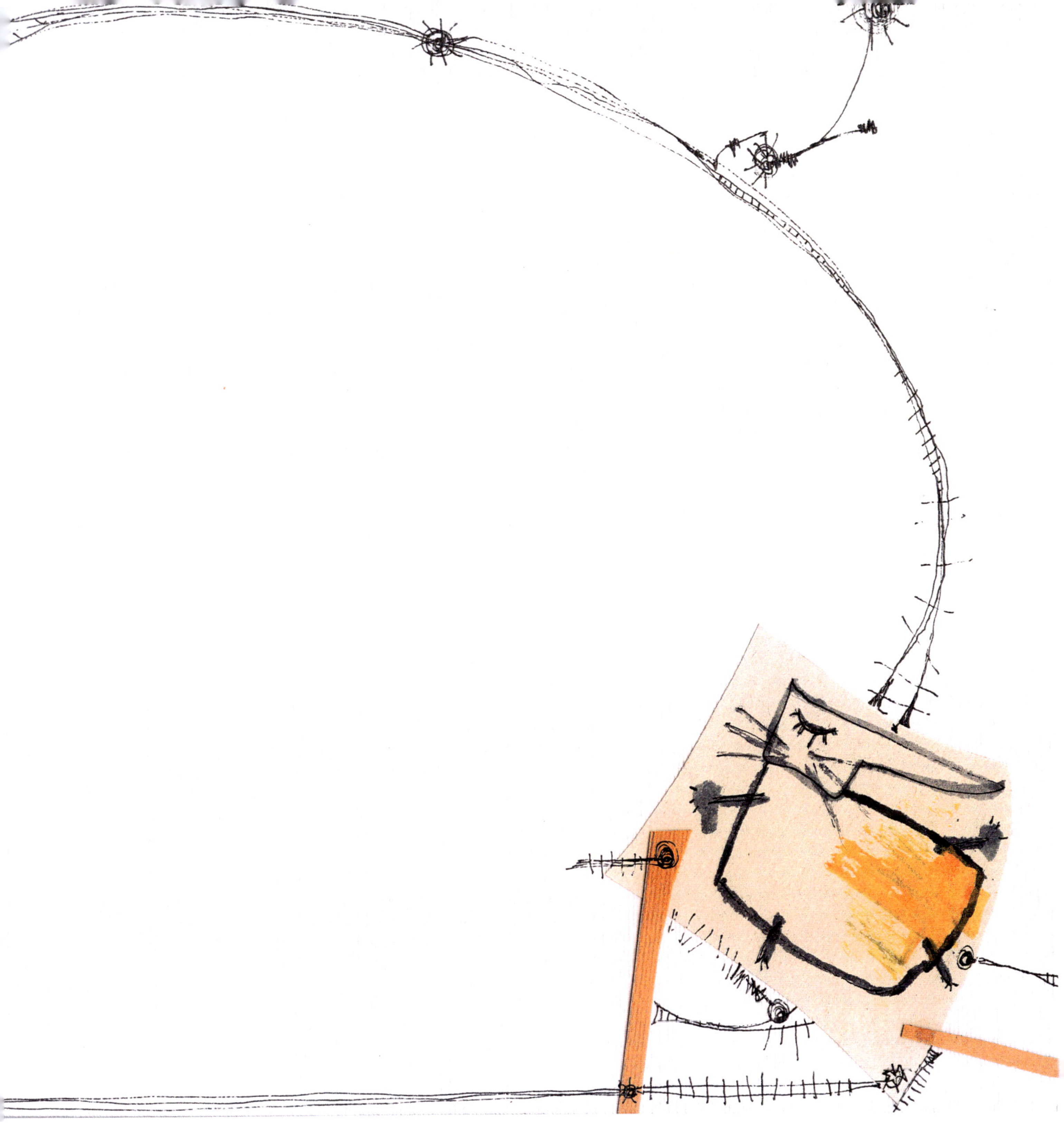

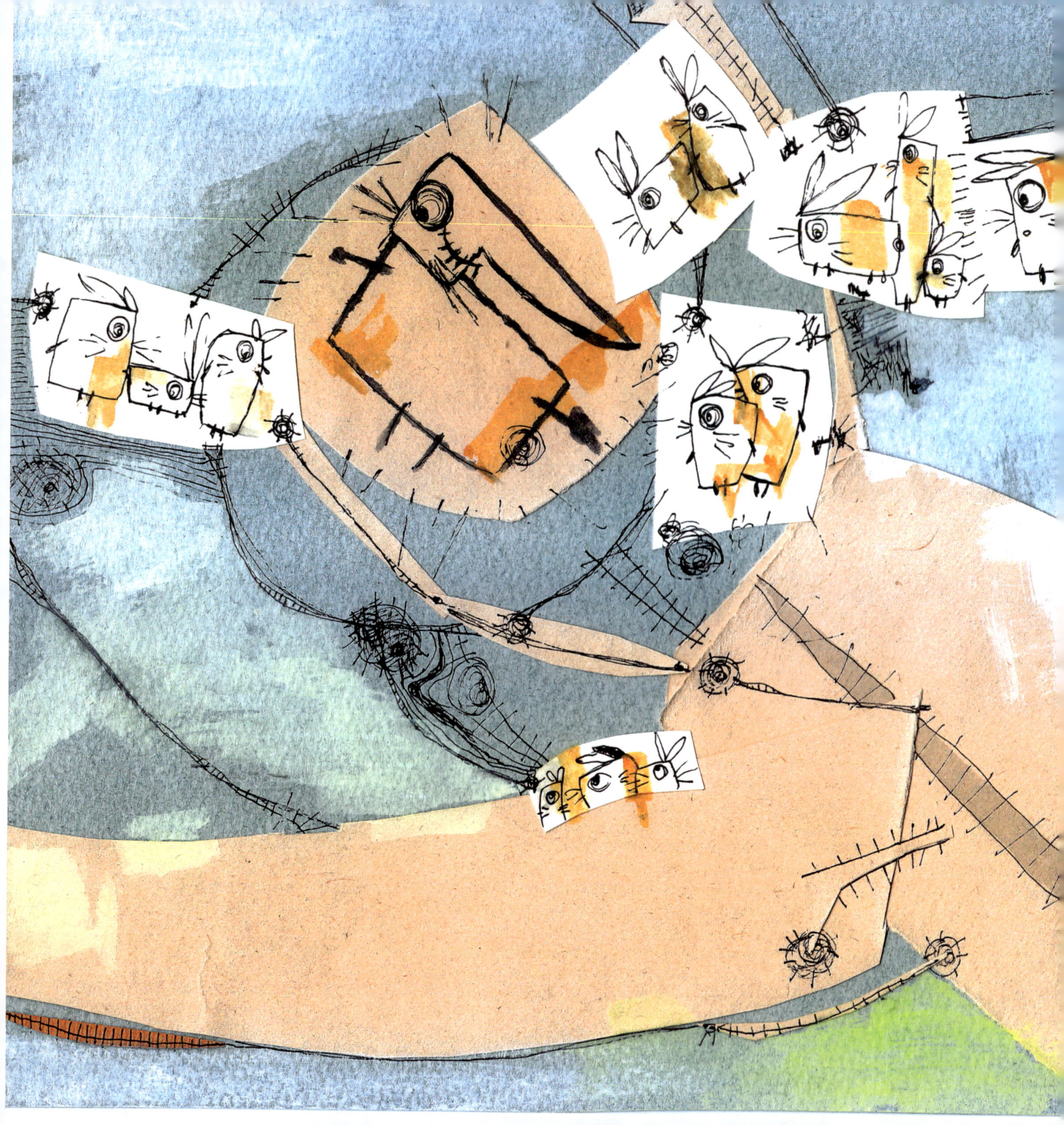

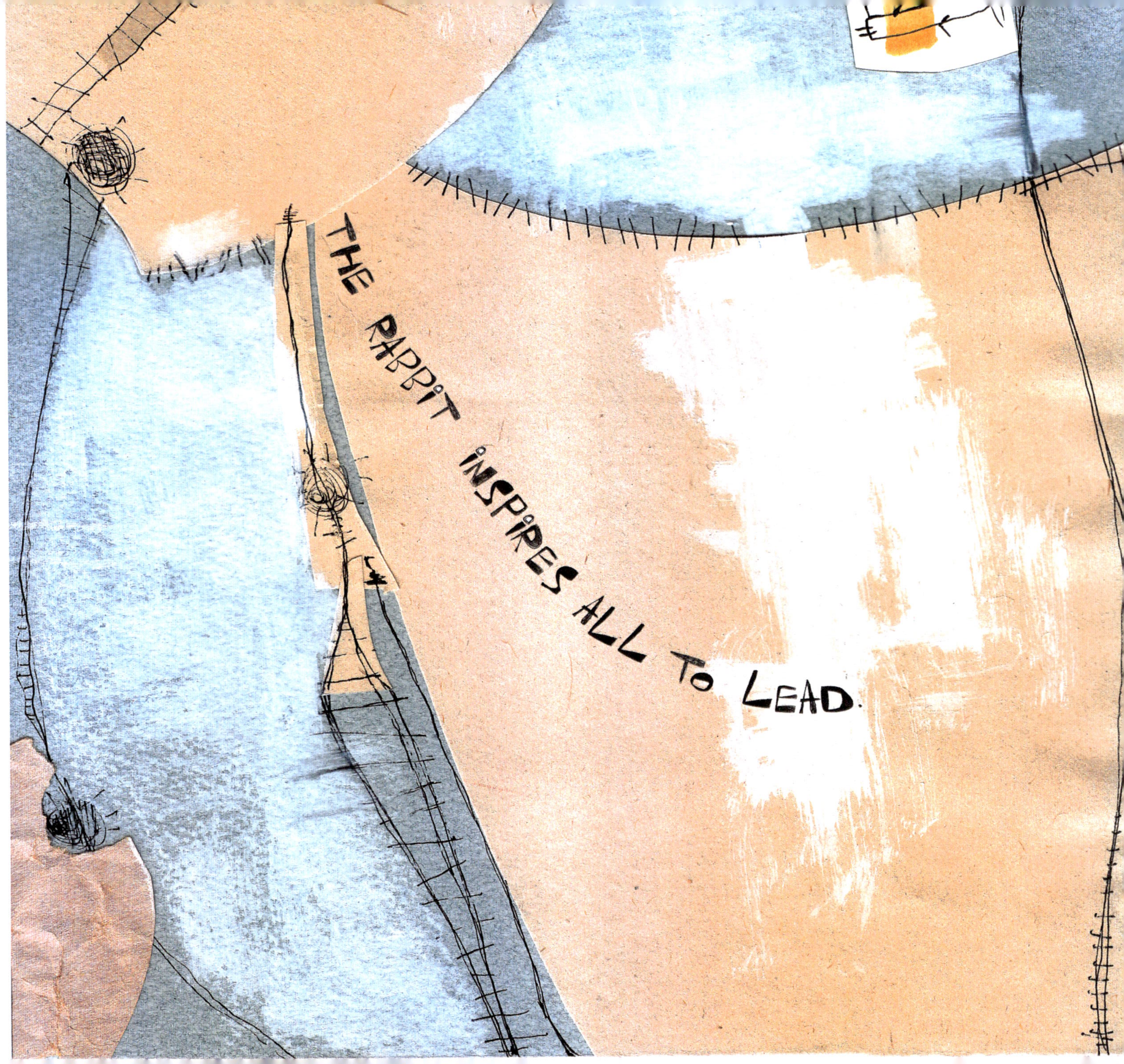

THE RABBIT INSPIRES ALL TO LEAD.

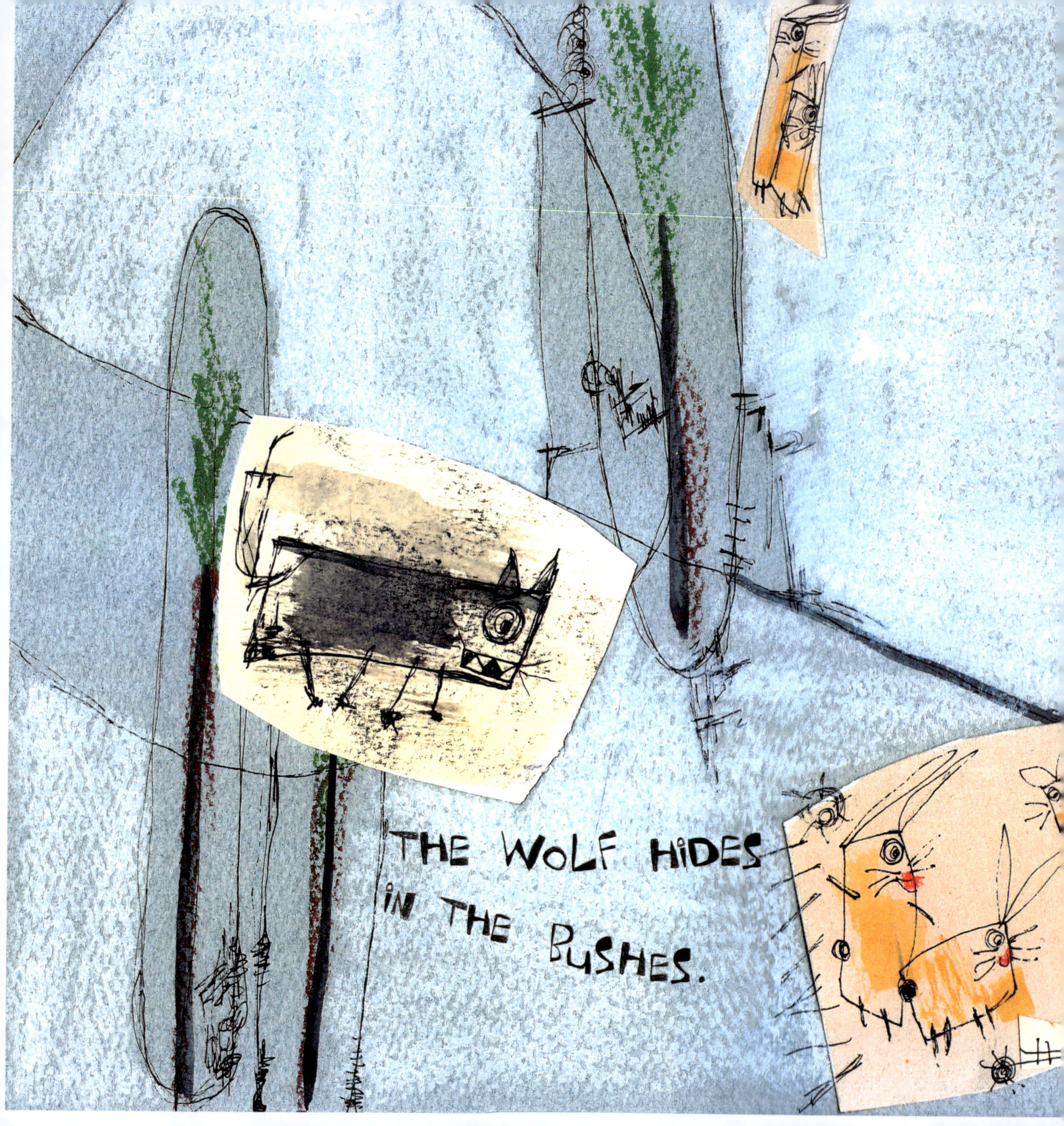
THE WOLF HIDES
IN THE BUSHES.

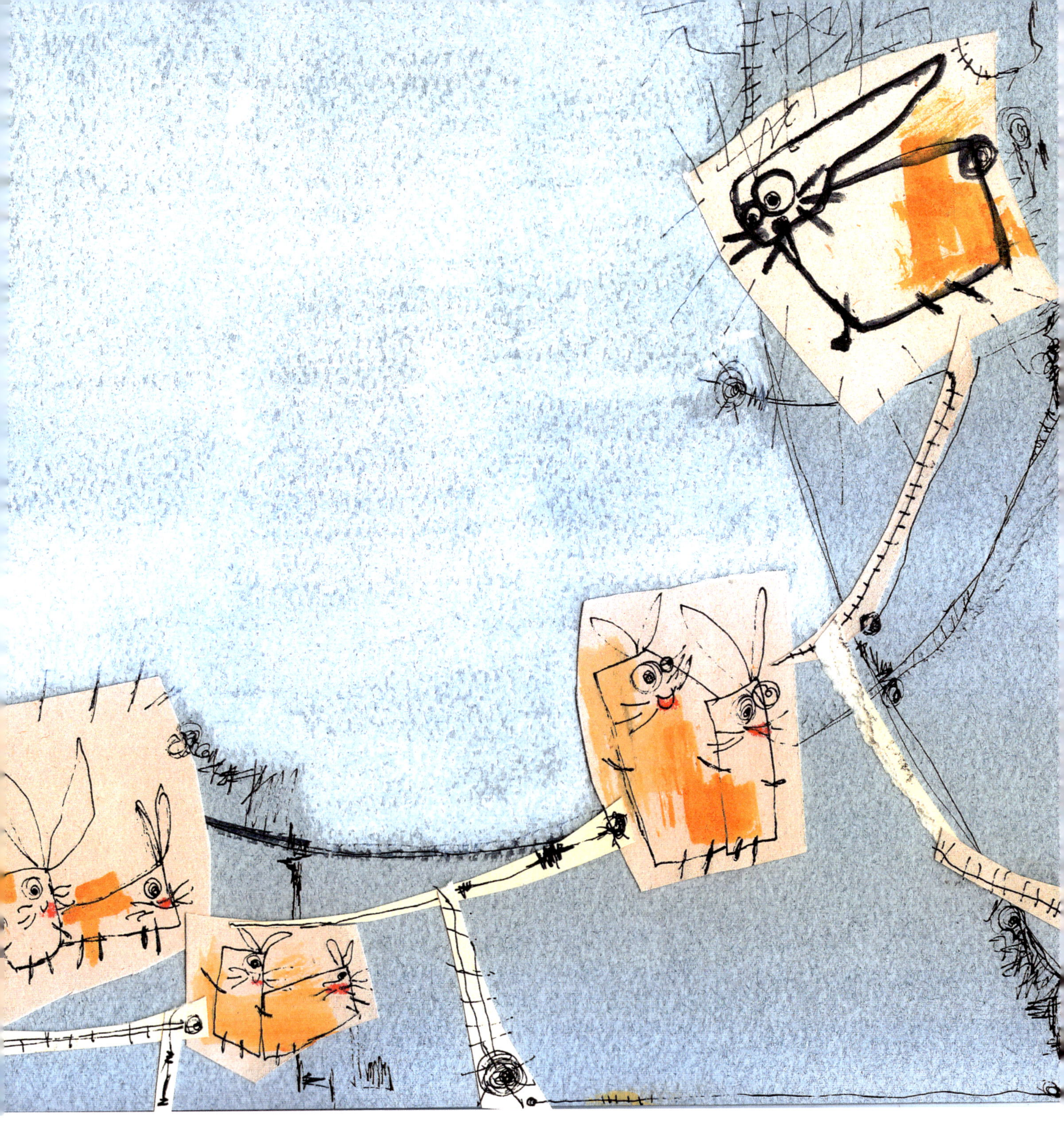

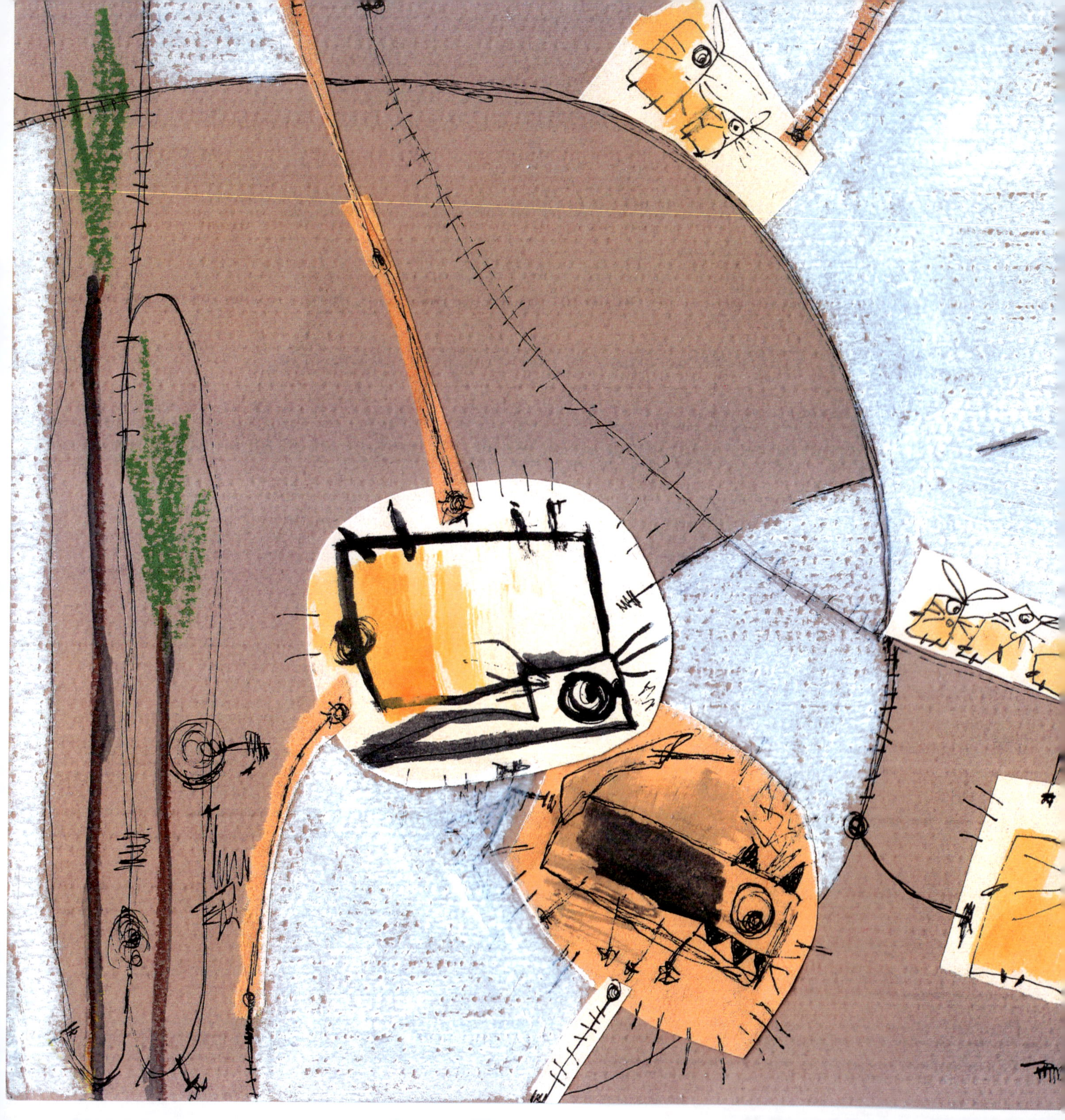

THE RABBIT SCARES THE WOLF AWAY.

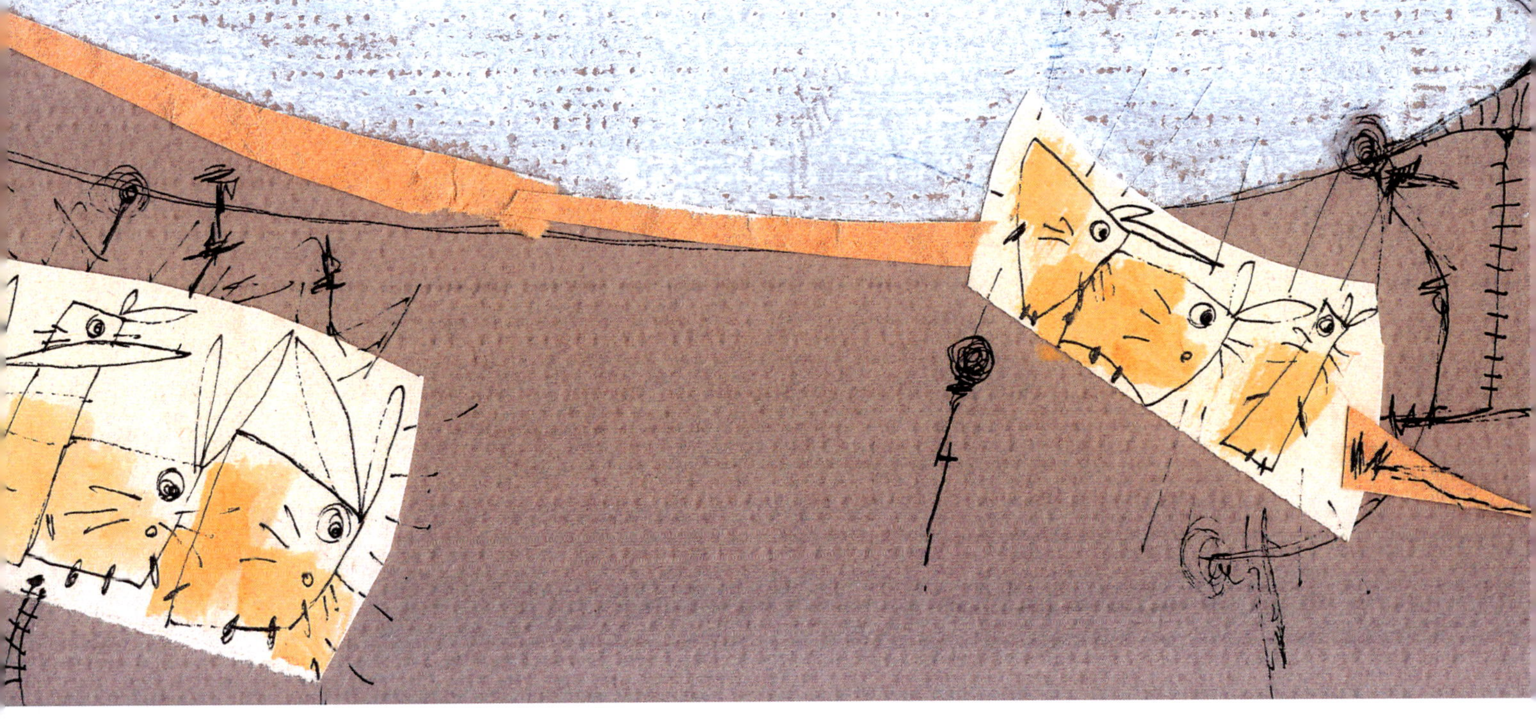

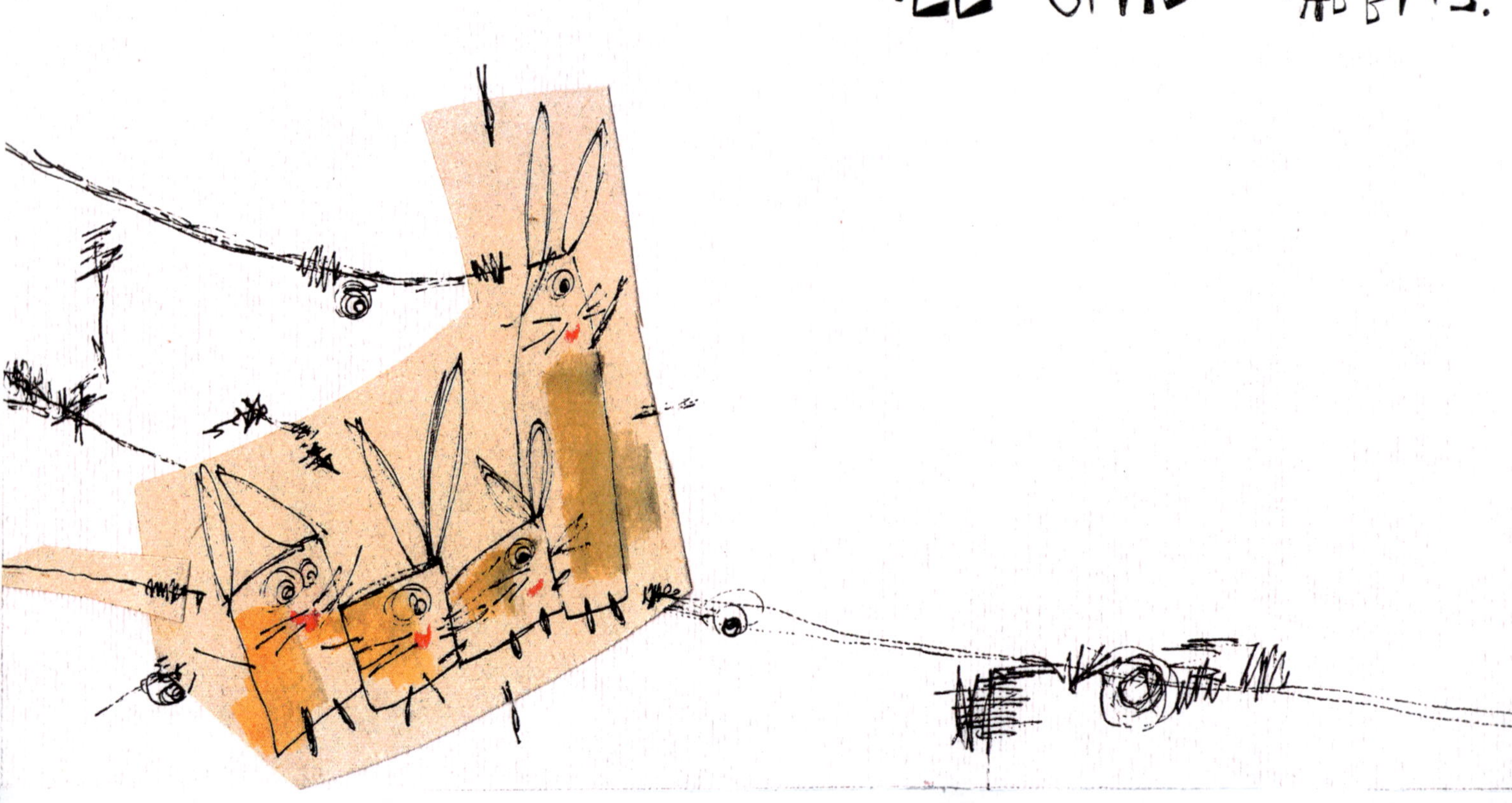

THE RABBIT WARNS ALL OTHER RABBITS.

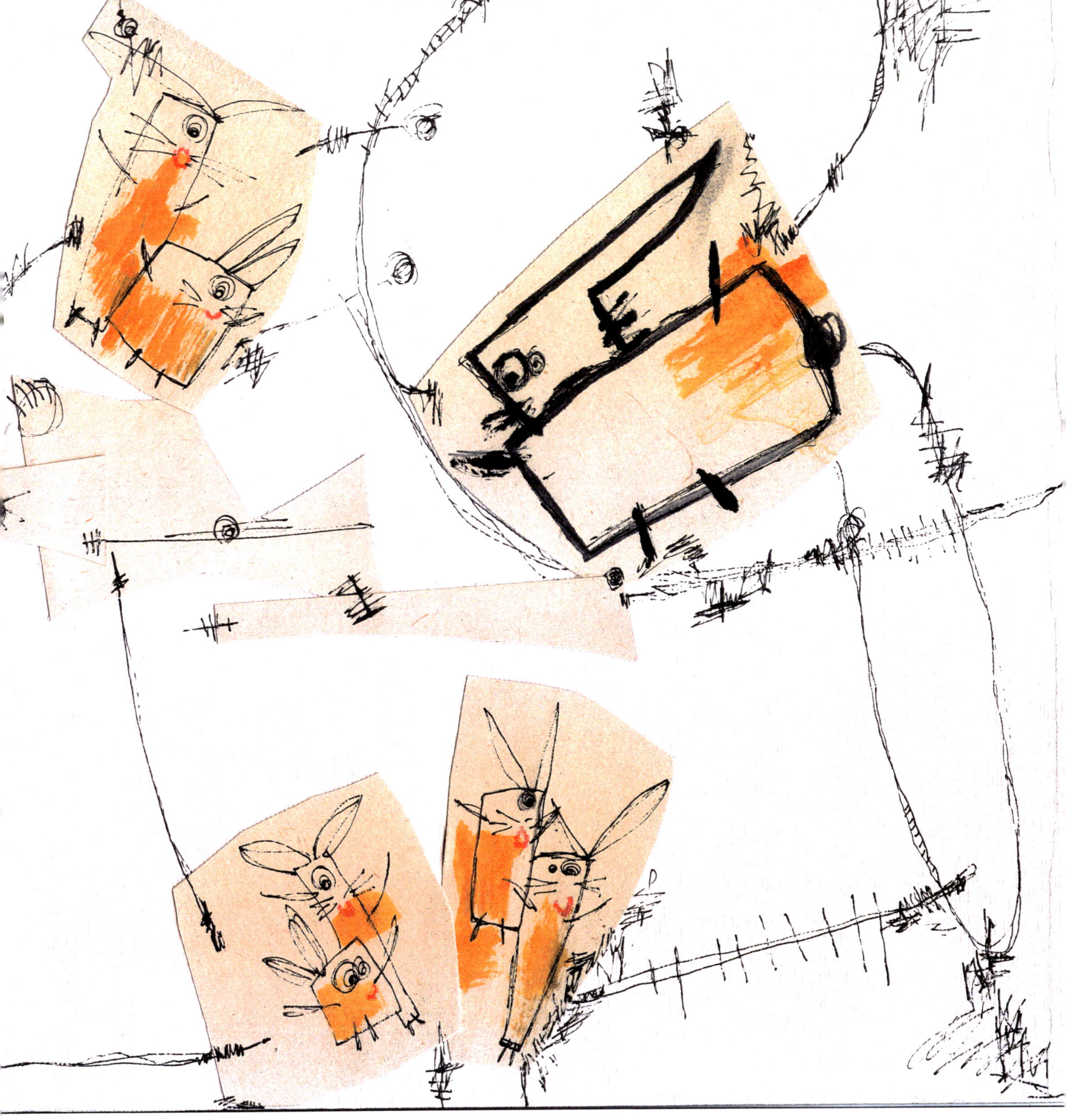

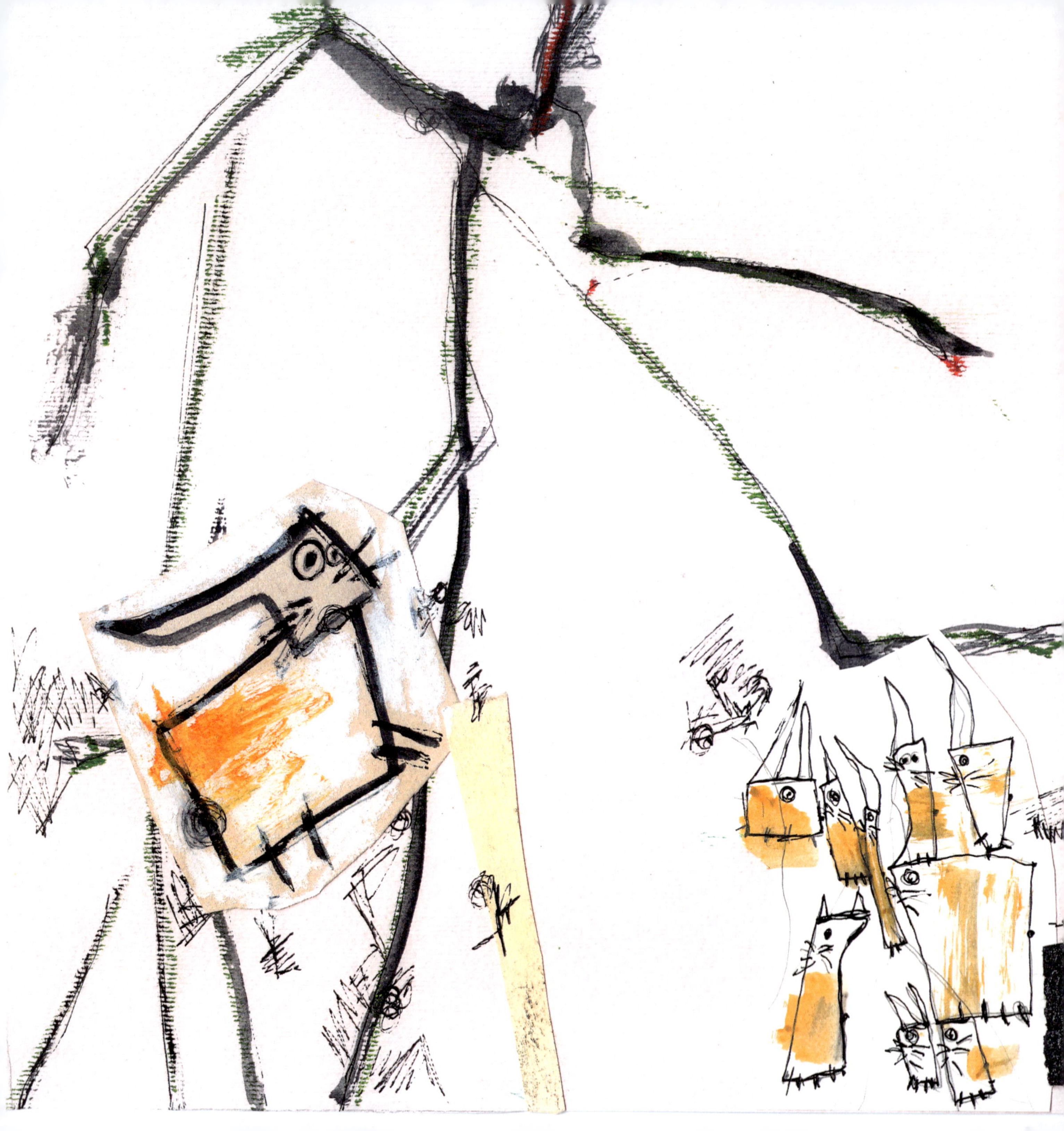

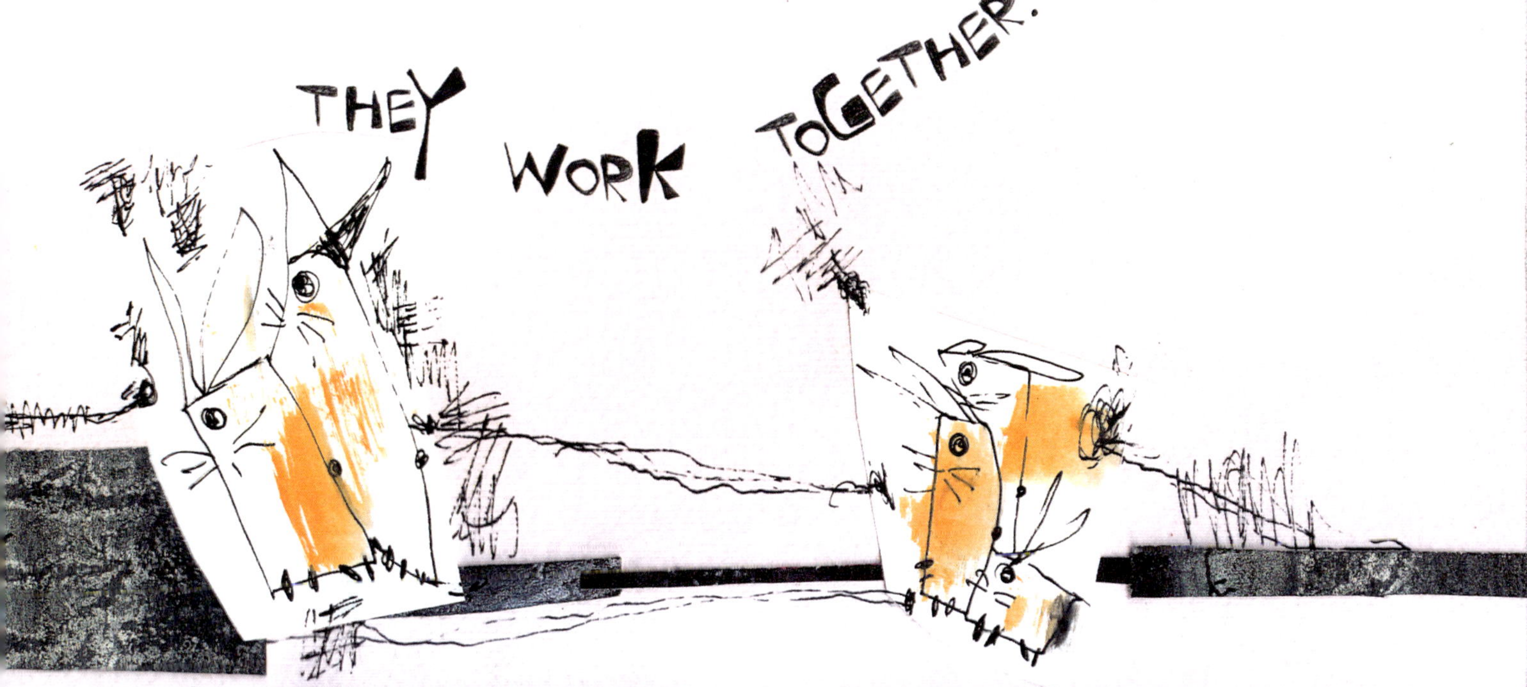

THEY WORK TOGETHER.

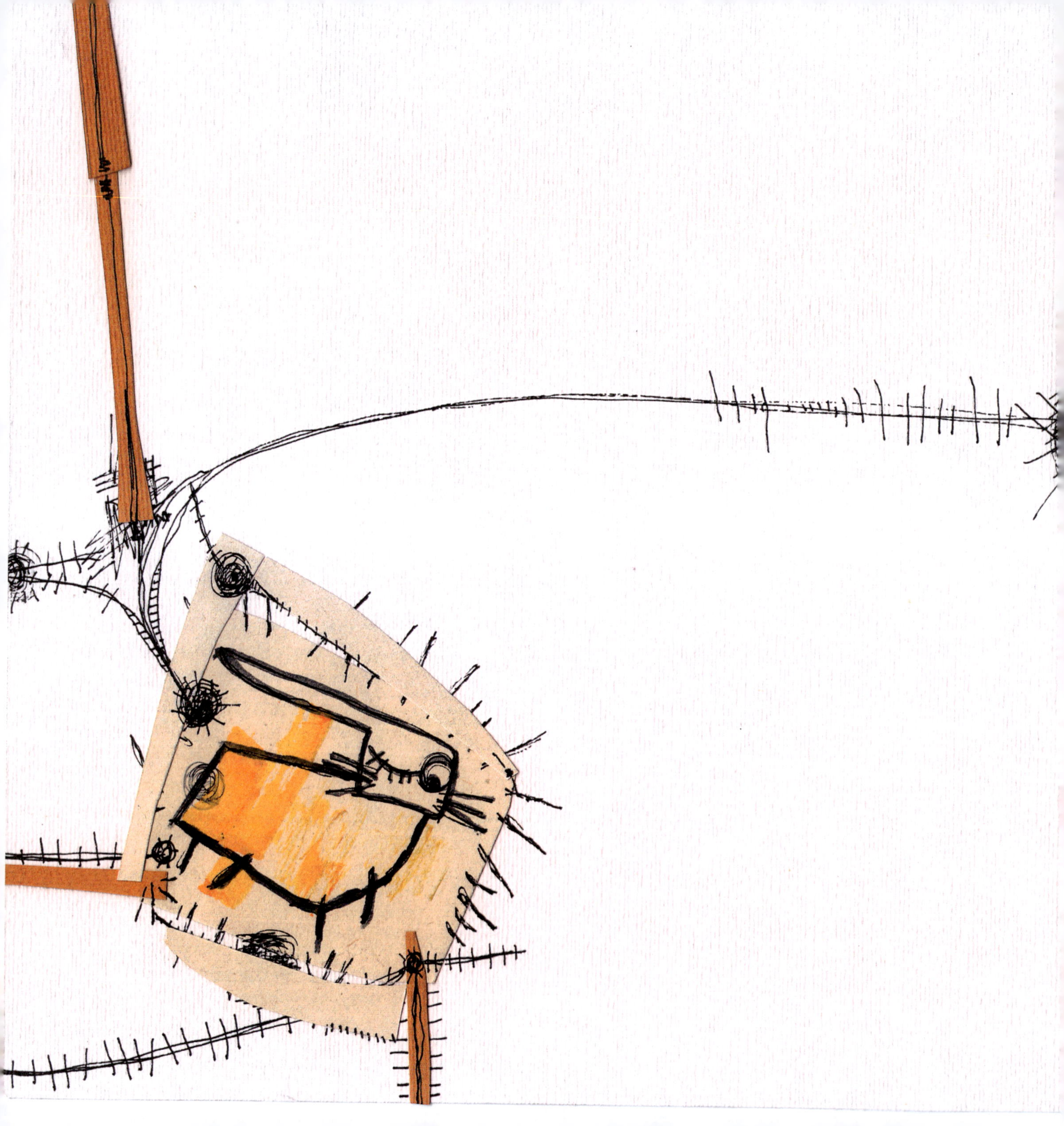

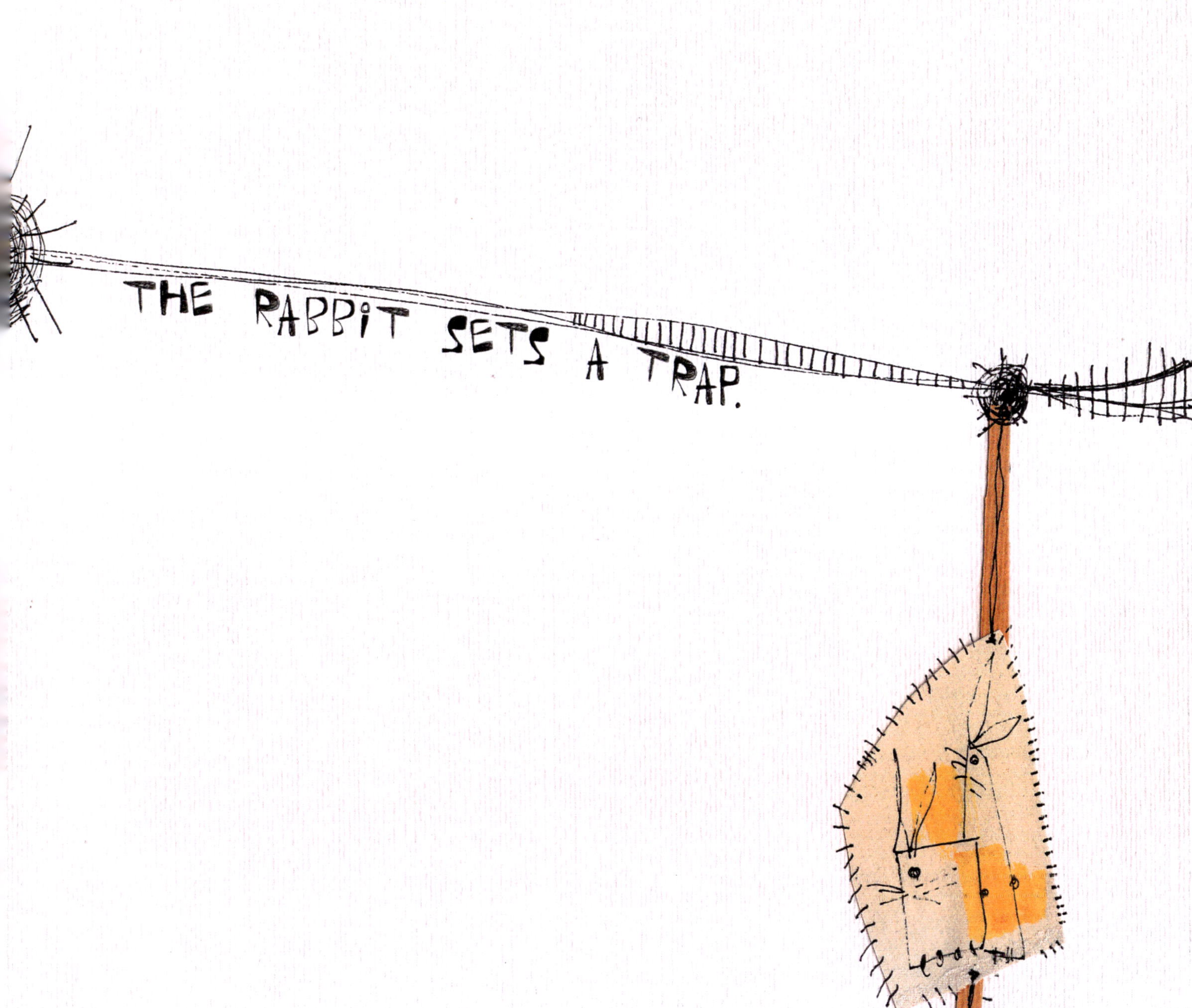
THE RABBIT SETS A TRAP.

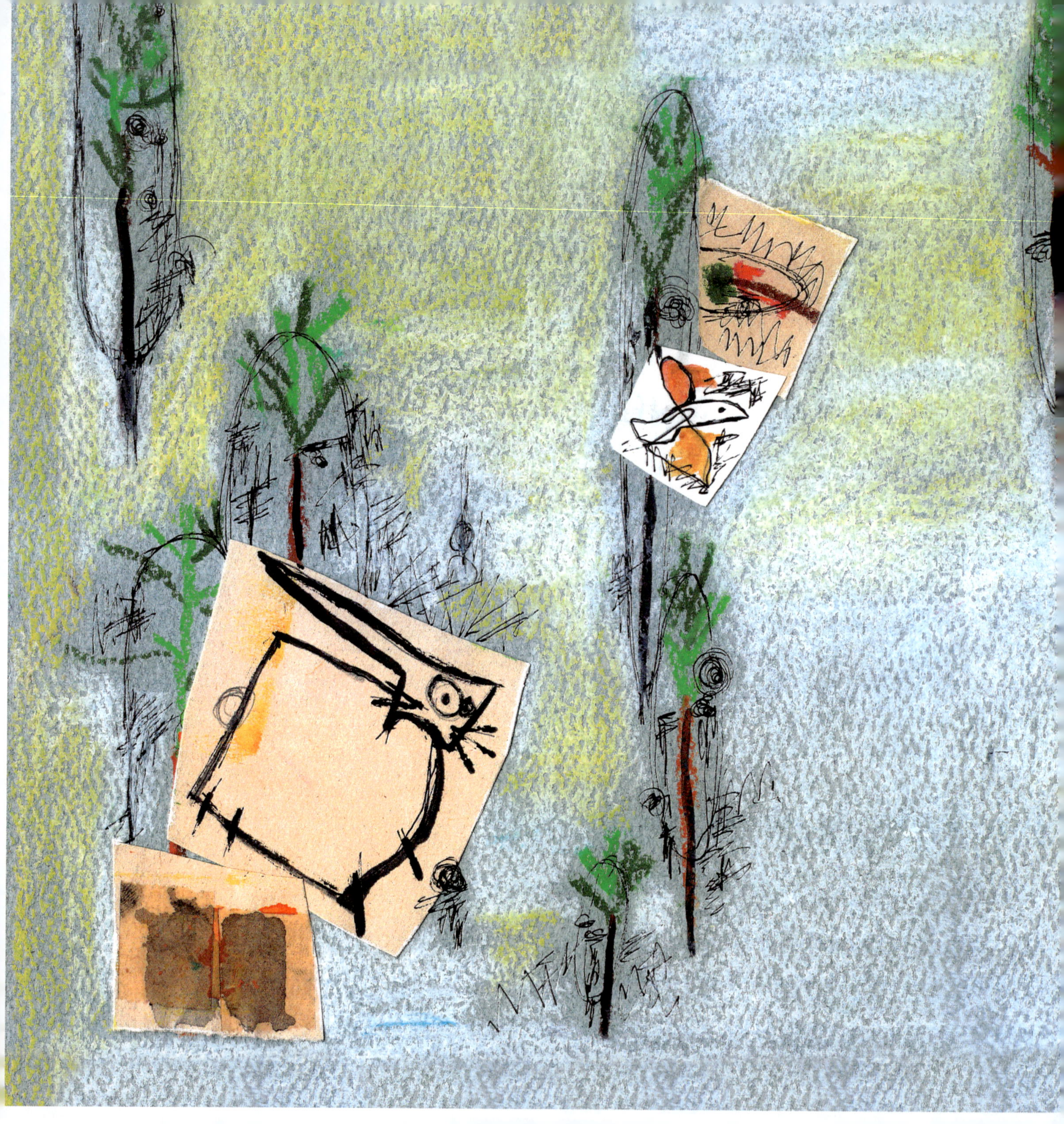

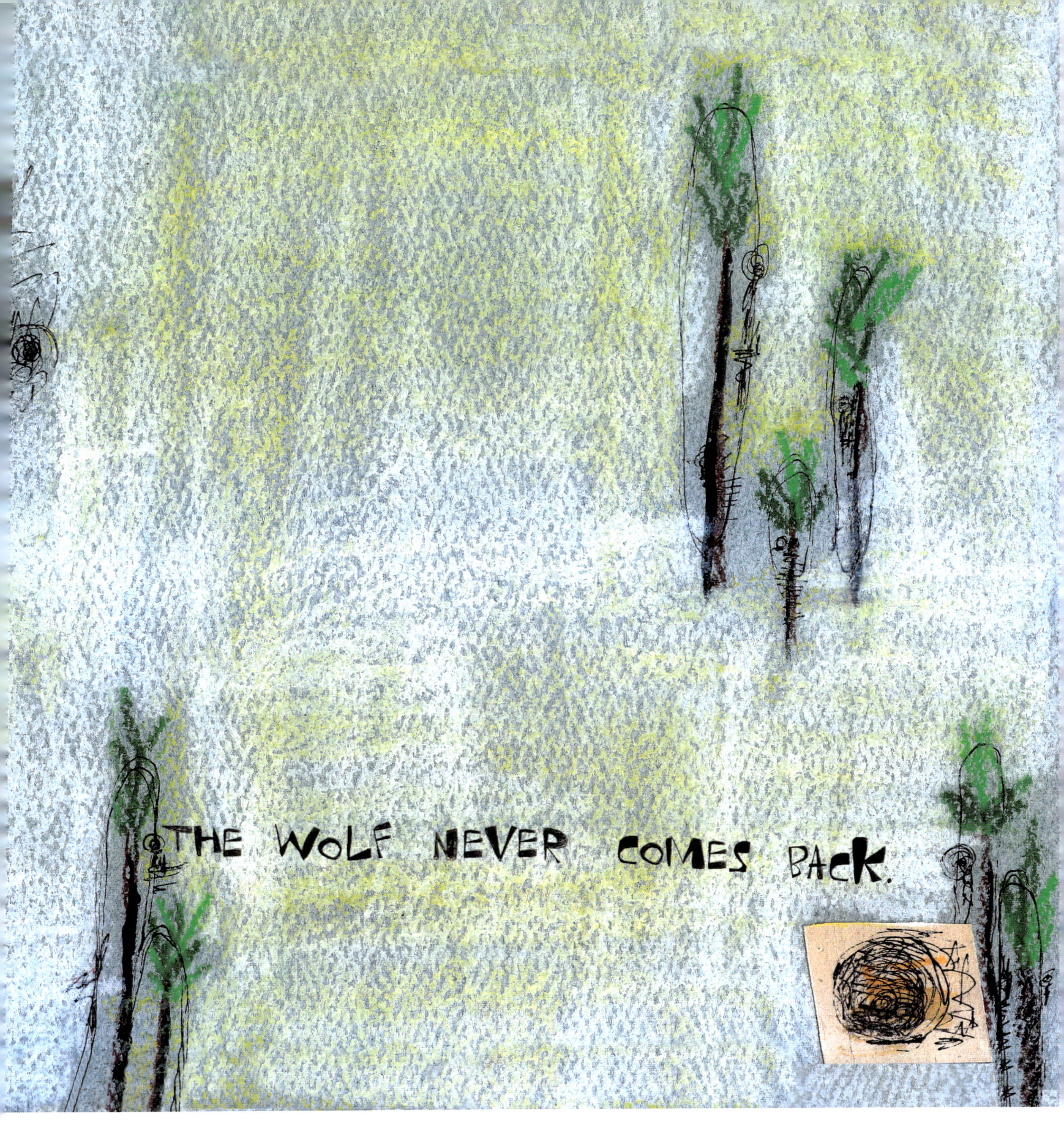
THE WOLF NEVER COMES BACK.

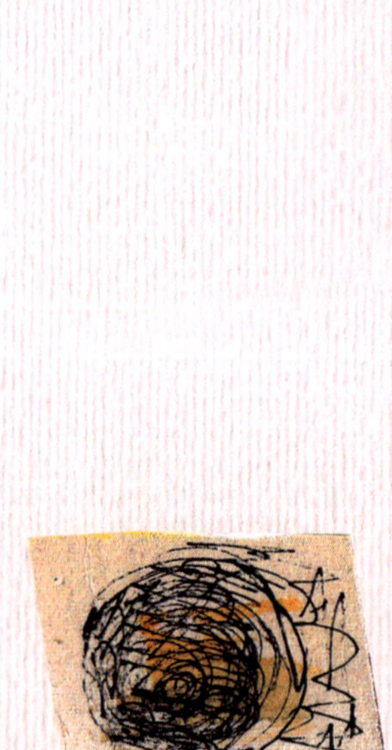

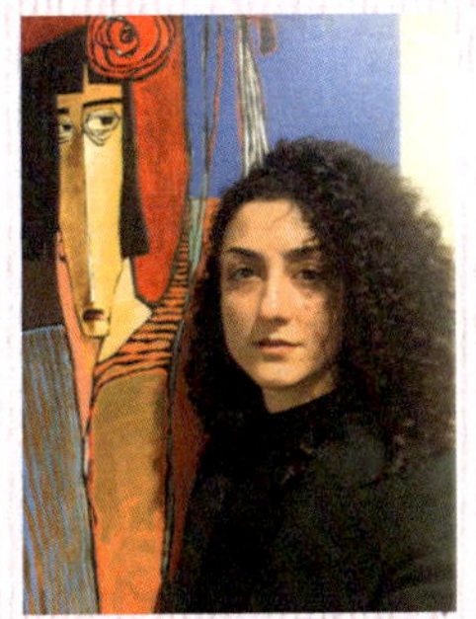

Bahar Taghiani is an illustrator and visual artist whose love for visual imagery began in early childhood. She started by creating characters out of pieces of paper, placing them in imagined stories, and bringing them to life. Today, her artworks are primarily created using mediums such as acrylic, collage, colored pencil, and watercolor, drawing inspiration from her perception of the world around her. Bahar is an award-winning artist, recognized by UNICEF for her illustration in the competition "Children on the Eve of New Year."

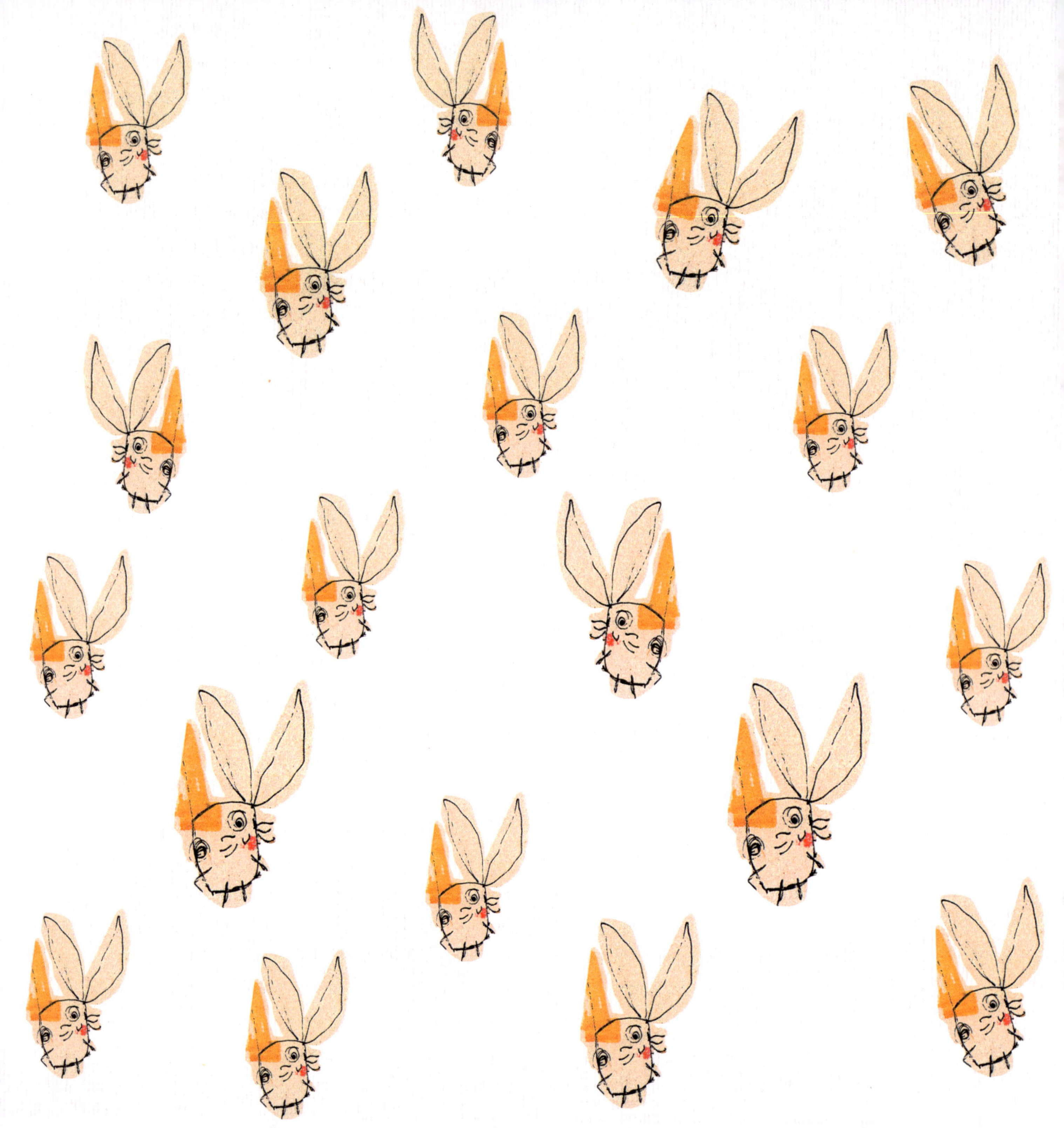

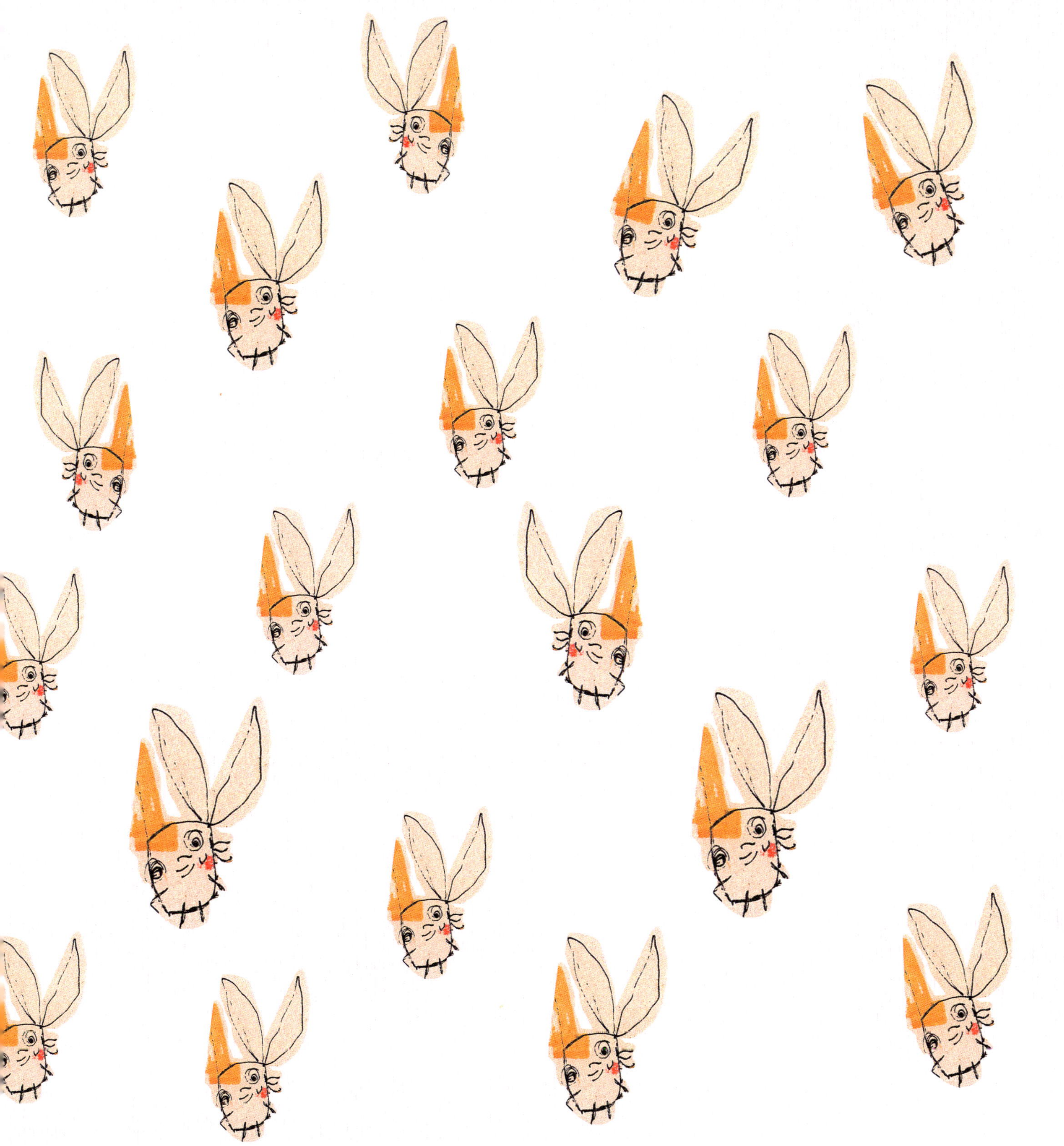

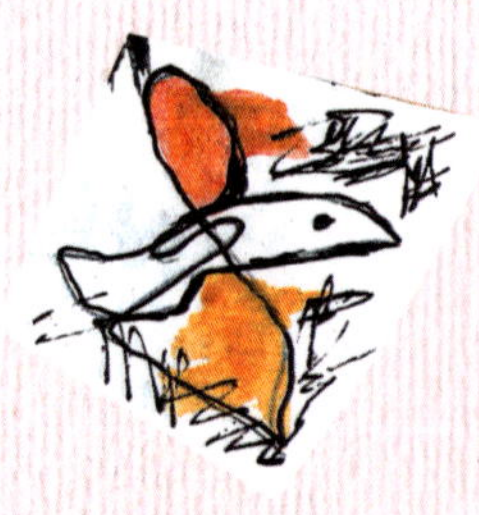

9 781763 818484